EXPOSED
LIGHTBULBS

FLATTERBY LIGHT BY INGO MAURER FOR INGO MAURER GMBH, 2016 Ten handmade butterflies flit around the lamp's oversized bulb in this limited-edition design (opposite).

E27 PENDANT LAMP BY MATTIAS STAHLBOM FOR MUUTO One of the most popular and simplest Nordic bulb sockets on the market, shown with Muuto's Fiber armchair designed by Iskos-Berlin (overleaf).

First published in 2017 by
Jacqui Small
An imprint of The Quarto Group
74–77 White Lion Street
London N1 9PF

Publisher **Jacqui Small**
Senior Commissioning Editor **Eszter Karpati**
Managing Editor **Emma Heyworth-Dunn**
Designer **Helen Bratby**
Editor **Sian Parkhouse**
Production **Maeve Healy**

ISBN: 9781911127260

A catalogue record for this book is available from the British Library.

2019 2018 2017
10 9 8 7 6 5 4 3 2 1

Printed in China

Quarto is the authority on a wide range of topics.
Quarto educates, entertains and enriches the lives of our readers – enthusiasts and lovers of hands-on living.
www.QuartoKnows.com

MIX
Paper from responsible sources
FSC® C104723

EXPOSED LIGHTBULBS

BRIGHT IDEAS FOR THE CONTEMPORARY INTERIOR

CHARLOTTE + PETER FIELL

acqui
mall

contents

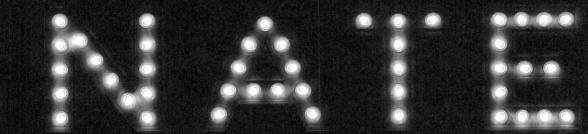

INATE

The story of the lightbulb

Within interior design there is a bit of a 'lightbulb moment' going on, quite literally, as people are increasingly waking up to the creative potential of a new generation of bulbs that can transform work, leisure and domestic spaces by giving them that all-important additional glow. Perhaps more than any designed object, the lightbulb is suffused with metaphor – its iconic form universally symbolizing bright ideas. Indeed, its distinctive outline has become a sort of glyphic shorthand for the whole notion of human thinking and the concept of genius. Yet at the same time the traditional 'standard' lightbulb is a potent signifier of industrial progress, while paradoxically also possessing a bygone resonance of a simpler, pre-digital age. For years the naked lightbulb's inherent glare meant it was often shrouded in light-filtering shades. However, over the last decade or so new kinds of bulbs that are intended to be left exposed have been introduced. Year-on-year, the choice of these types of illuminants has diversified and grown, as has their potential to be used in interesting ways within contemporary interiors – which is the reason for this book, as the coming pages attest. Today, there are a plethora of lightbulb types to choose from, ranging from Edisonian vintage-style ones that can give a room an instant Steampunk nostalgia or Hipster retro-industrial feel to state-of-the-art designs that have shed the historic form of the traditional lightbulb for something altogether more sculptural and spectacular. Twinned with this, there have always been an array of acknowledged – and indeed timeless – design icons that have exploited the magical potential of exposed bulbs, but to these have been added in recent years a new and widening crop of bulb-revealing lighting designs that similarly celebrate that most glorious ordinary-yet-transformative invention of the man-made world – the electrifying lightbulb.

SP1000 BRASS SOCKET This funnel-shaped cover by House Doctor is the perfect welcoming light for an entrance space (opposite).

37

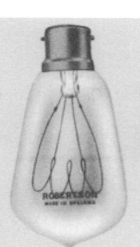

40

41

38

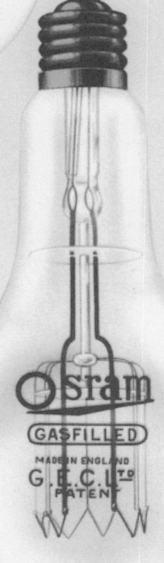

The spark
of a bright idea

Of all mankind's great inventions, the lightbulb is the one most associated with the dawning of the electric age. At the flip of a switch it changed human history, turning dark into light. Safe, clean, cheap and practical, it was quite simply the miracle of the modern age, which not only effectively lengthened the day but has also helped to shape our lives ever since. It was not until the early 19th century that the first steps towards a form of flameless illumination were taken by the British scientist Humphry Davy, when he famously demonstrated the world's first electric carbon-arc experiment at the Royal Institution in London in 1809. Using two carbon rods placed close to each other, but not touching, Davy ran an electric current through them, which caused, according to fellow scientist Michael Faraday, 'a brilliant ascending arch of light' when the electric charge sparked bridge-like across the gap between them to complete its circuit. It would, however, take another 30 years before Davy's technology was commercialized and even then the glaring brightness of arc lighting meant it had no practical application within the domestic environment, and was, therefore, only suitable for street, stadium and factory lighting, as it still is.

This inherent and blinding flaw led other scientists and inventors to cast around for another form of flameless electric lighting that would be kinder on the eye. In 1820, Warren de la Rue demonstrated the principle of platinum incandescence, while another

EARLY LAMPS An original Osram catalogue shows the company's different incandescent models (opposite). Original postcard designed by F. Schoen, c. 1908, advertising Wolfram (tungsten filament) lightbulbs (above).

early incandescent lighting experiment was outlined in an article by William Robert Grove that was published in *Philosophical Magazine* in 1840. This new experiment in lighting technology relied on a coiled filament of platinum attached at either end to two charged copper wires, encased in a glass tumbler partially submerged in a bowl of water. The air was pumped out to produce a somewhat imperfect vacuum, which nevertheless helped to retard the destruction of the incandescent filament from oxidation, produced when a charge of electricity was run through it to produce a glowing heat. This simple, yet at the time, presumably spectacular experiment was the progenitor of today's modern lightbulb, and sparked a race among various inventors to become the first to commercialize this ground-breaking technology. In fact, it would take another three decades of research and development to turn this bright idea into a practical lighting solution that would change people's everyday lives. In 1841 – the year following the publication of Grove's paper – Frederick de Moleyns was granted the first British patent for incandescent lighting, with his invention consisting of two coils of platinum set in a vacuum bulb. Another early pioneer was a young American called John Wellington Starr, who moved to London and, with the help of Faraday, obtained a British patent in 1845 for two styles of lamp. One employed a platinum strip encased in a non-vacuum glass enclosure; the other utilized a carbon strip held between two metal clamps in a glass-encased vacuum, obtained by using a mercury column. Significantly, this latter configuration meant that when the carbon strip degraded, it could be replaced, which in effect made Starr's lamp renewable.

The inventor William Edwards Staite was also an early trailblazing advocate of incandescent lighting technology and gave several lectures on the subject, which importantly the young

MONSTER BULB Original press photograph showing a giant Japanese-made lightbulb that could provide 50 kilowatts of illumination, 1962.

Joseph Swan attended and was inspired by. Indeed, over the succeeding years, Swan never lost his interest in this potentially life-changing technology. Like others working in this field, he realized that the key to making a successful lightbulb lay in being able to produce a perfect vacuum because otherwise any metal or carbon filament just oxidized too quickly. The only problem was that it was impossible to achieve such a vacuum, until the German-born chemist Hermann Sprengel invented his eponymous vacuum pump in 1865 while he was working in London. Using this kind of pump, Swan was able to expel enough air from a bulb of glass to create the first practical incandescent lightbulb in 1878, which he publically demonstrated the following year to the Newcastle Chemical Society. He did not, however, apply for a patent to protect his invention until 1880 – which meant that the American inventor, Thomas Alva Edison, was able to pip him to the post by filing two patents: the first for 'Improvements to Electric Lights' in October 1878, and the second for the design of a practical incandescent 'Electric-Lamp' with a carbonized filament in November 1879. So while Swan might have been the first to invent the first practical incandescent electric lightbulb, it was Edison who actually devised the first lightbulb design to be commercialized. In fact, by 1880, both Edison and Swan held patents for their respective incandescent lamps, and the ensuing litigation was resolved by the establishment of a joint company, known as Ediswan, in 1883. A little-known fact about lightbulb fittings is that it was Swan who devised the bayonet fitting, whereas Edison opted for a screw cap – which is why, even to this day, there are two systems in some countries. During the mid- to late-19th century there were a host of other inventors, including William Sawyer and Hiram Maxim, who were also working within this field.

The lighting wizard of Menlo Park

Crucially, as a gifted inventor-entrepreneur, Edison did not just design the first commercially successful lightbulb, but devised a complete power-delivery system and then rolled out the entire electric grid, so that electric lighting could be used in factories, offices and homes across America and Europe, and eventually throughout the world. No wonder, therefore, the lightbulb is so closely associated with not only the genius of invention, but also the rise of the modern electrical age. Famously, Edison and his research team, which was nicknamed the 'Insomnia Squad', had arrived at the final design of his practical electric lightbulb through a painstaking iterative approach to research and development, which involved thousands of trial-and-error experiments, each testing a slightly new design refinement. Although the exact number of experiments undertaken at the Menlo Park laboratory is unknown, it was probably around 3,000, rather than the 10,000 so frequently cited. In an interview in *Harper's Monthly* magazine in 1890, Edison observed, 'I have constructed three thousand different theories in connection with the electric light, each one of them

reasonable and apparently to be true. Yet only in two cases did my experiments prove the truth of my theory. My chief difficulty, as perhaps you know, was in constructing the carbon filament, the incandescence of which is the source of the light. Every quarter of the globe was ransacked by my agents, and all sorts of the queerest materials were used, until finally the shred of bamboo now utilized was settled upon. Even now, I am still at work nearly every day on the lamp.'

UPPER FLOOR, EDISON'S MENLO PARK LABORATORY, DEARBORN, MICH.

THOMAS EDISON The world-changing incandescent lightbulb, described by one commentator as 'the little gadget which lights the world', was developed at the research laboratory at Menlo Park.

Over the coming years and decades, Edison's firm, General Electric Company (GEC) – along with other firms (including Swan's) – made innumerable technological advances within the field of electric lighting.

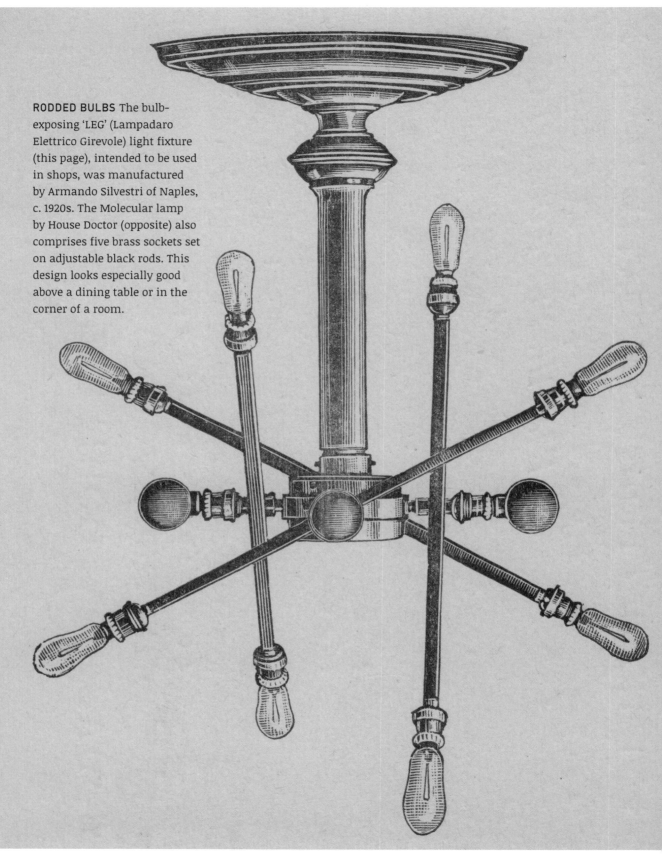

RODDED BULBS The bulb-exposing 'LEG' (Lampadaro Elettrico Girevole) light fixture (this page), intended to be used in shops, was manufactured by Armando Silvestri of Naples, c. 1920s. The Molecular lamp by House Doctor (opposite) also comprises five brass sockets set on adjustable black rods. This design looks especially good above a dining table or in the corner of a room.

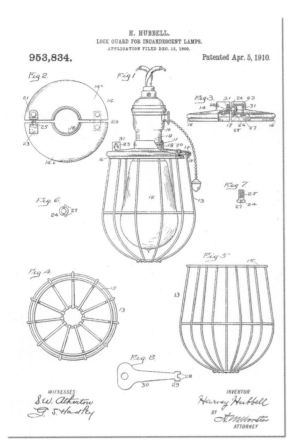

H. HUBBELL.
LOCK GUARD FOR INCANDESCENT LAMPS.
APPLICATION FILED DEC. 13, 1909.

953,834.

Patented Apr. 5, 1910.

METAL CAGES US Patent drawing of
'Lock Guard for Incandescent Lamps'
filed by Harvey Hubbell II, 1909.

Improvements + advances

When the electric lightbulb was first introduced, lamps were often designed to show off this marvel of the modern electric age. The Café Museum, designed by Adolf Loos in Vienna in 1899, was a glorious example of how bare lightbulbs could be used to spectacular glittering effect within a space, which was starkly minimal for its day. Many other early lighting designs similarly functioned as vehicles for the display of this new wondrous invention. However, the novelty of leaving bulbs bare soon wore off, especially when in 1908 the first ductile tungsten filament lightbulbs appeared, which not only lasted longer than their cellulose-filament forebears, but were also significantly brighter. Eventually, as a result of this new lightbulb technology, which had been developed by William David Coolidge at GEC, the naked lightbulb was consigned mainly to industrial usage – in factories and the like – while in the home the use of light-diffusing shades made of fabric, opalescent glass or metal became de rigueur.

Indeed, the utlization of bare lightbulbs was for the most part associated with utilitarian factory lighting, which often featured exposed bulbs set in protective 'shock-proof' metal cages – a style genre that has made a surprising but definite comeback over the last few years, thanks to its evocative pre-digital industrial connotations.

CAFÉ MUSEUM, VIENNA Designed by
Adolf Loos in 1899, the remarkably
forward-looking modern interior
featured exposed lightbulbs.

Irving Langmuir devised another improvement in lighting technology in 1913, which involved filling bulbs with nitrogen gas to increase the lifespan of their tungsten filaments, which helped retard their oxidization. While in 1925, Marvin Pipkin, working at GEC, created the first 'frosted' lightbulbs, whereby the bulbs internal surfaces were treated with hydrofluoric acid. This etching method helped to diffuse the glare of a bare lightbulb considerably. Another development in lightbulb technology occurred around 1930, when double-coiled tungsten filament bulbs were commercially introduced, which not only helped to give the filaments great durability, and thereby longevity, but also provided more uniform luminescence. Eventually in 1947, Pipkin came up with an even better method of 'frosting' lightbulbs that employed a powdered silica coating process, which made them even softer on the eye. Thanks to Pipkin's improved 'frosting' method, bare lightbulbs became fashionable once more within domestic interiors – with various on-trend sputnik-like fixtures attesting to this fact. During this postwar period, coloured lightbulbs in modish pastel tints also became popular, as they were seen as having, according to Westinghouse's publicity, 'flattering decorative effects'. Notwithstanding, however, the exposed bulb was still not accepted widely, as the romantically inclined Blanche DuBois observed in Tennessee Williams's 1947 play, *A Streetcar Named Desire*: 'I can't stand a naked lightbulb, any more than I can a rude remark or a vulgar action' – which pretty much summed up the general consensus of the time.

TECHNOLOGICAL LEAPS Carl W. Mitman, curator of engineering at the Smithsonian Institution, with the first cold electric light bulb, 1924 (left).

QUALITY CONTROL Operator Louis Barbow checks the standards of lightbulbs on this machine devised by the US National Bureau of Standards, 1938 (right).

OUTSIZED GLOBES These stunning, large bulb-like ceiling lights are used to illuminate Otto Wagner's Karlsplatz Stadtbahn station in Vienna (opened 1899).

PENDANTS A Viennese sitting area in a hallway designed by J. Demetz in 1929, illuminated with a simple bulb-like globe (this page). These contemporary blobular bulbs (opposite) – Form pendants by Form Us With Love for Design House Stockholm – are 'borrowed from the timeless world of the industrial lightbulb'.

Creative experimentation + technological leaps

From the mid the 1950s onwards, Italian designer Achille Castiglioni experimented with different types of exposed lightbulbs to create a number of spectacular designs – including his iconic Luminator floorlamp, the Taraxacum chandelier made from a tight cluster of transparent bulbs and his Toio floorlamp that cleverly incorporated a 300-watt car headlamp specially imported from the United States. During the 1960s and 1970s, various designers, including the likes of Vico Magistretti, Olivier Mourgue and Verner Panton, created sculptural lighting designs that similarly employed exposed lightbulbs to dramatic effect. This period also saw designers begin to experiment creatively with halogen bulbs – first invented in 1953 – which are lighter and more compact than tungsten bulbs, and have a luminescence that is quite orangey, and more tonally akin to sunlight. However, while dazzlingly bright halogen bulbs might be perfect for spotlighting, they also have one major Achilles heel: they get extremely hot – which makes them relatively unstable and liable to explode if handled too much.

During the '60s and '70s, designers also explored the potential of fluorescent lighting tubes, which had first come onto the market in 1938. However, because of their inherent eye-wearying, flickering and cold-toned brightness, the resulting designs most often diffused the emitted light using screening shields of colourful or white opalescent acrylic. The next big thing in lighting technology was the advent of LEDs (light-emitting diodes), with the world's first visible-spectrum LED being invented by Nick Holonyak Jr, while he

JUGENDSTIL CHANDELIER This stunning cascade of bulbs is used to illuminate Otto Wagner's Steinhof Church in Vienna, built 1904–07.

FROM FLUORESCENT TO LED Fluorescent lighting tubes being inspected during their manufacture, 1941 (right). Light Structure hanging/table light by Peter Hamburger and Ingo Maurer for Ingo Maurer GmbH, 1970/2013 (far right), is a Constructivist-style lighting assemblage of six LED lighting tubes. It originally used fluorescent bulbs when it was first introduced.

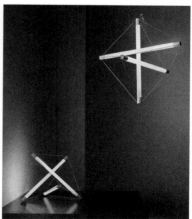

was working at General Electric's research laboratory in Syracuse, New York, in 1962. This very first LED was red in colour. However, a decade later, one of Holonyak's students, M. George Craford, invented not only a brighter red LED, but also the world's very first yellow LED. Craford's pioneering research was followed in 1976 with another major advancement in LED technology by Thomas P. Pearsall, who developed a much brighter kind of light-emitting diode. It was, however, Shuji Nakamura, while working for the Nichia Corporation, who perhaps made the biggest breakthrough with his invention of the first high-brightness gallium nitride (GaN) LED, whose brilliant blue light could be converted to a more visually acceptable and functional practical yellow tone by means of a multi-layered coating. Initially far too expensive to put into large-scale mass-production, the first commercially manufactured blue-light LEDs were eventually launched in 1994. And although their luminescence was starkly white in tone, they more than made up for this tonal deficiency with their cooler energy efficiency – indeed, today's colour-improved LEDs cost fives times less to run than conventional incandescent bulbs.

HANGING TUBES Fluorescent lighting (above) is used in an innovative way by Danish design brand Hay, to showcase its innovative Nobody felt chair.

CHANDELIERS Watercolour of the drawing room in Charles Robert Ashbee's house, at 35 Cheyne Walk, London, c. 1895 (opposite), incorporating a stunning beaten metal chandelier to Ashbee's design, with hanging exposed lightbulbs. Carousel pendant light by Lee Broom (this page) features 30 gunmetal polished cylinders each housing an inset LED bulb in order to create a playful ring of light.

Today's state of lighting play

The marked energy efficiency of LEDs has since driven governments across the world to implement legislation that has seen the controversial phasing out of traditional incandescent tungsten-filament lightbulbs for general lighting purposes over the last decade or so. This widespread ban has, in turn, pushed manufacturers to bring on stream all kinds of alternative, more eco-efficient lightbulbs, including low-energy halogen, LED, compact fluorescent and magnetic induction. This increased research activity has not only made LEDs a lot cheaper than they used to be, but also led to a veritable cornucopia of choices, from the strictly utilitarian to a host of design-statement lightbulbs. For the first time in its history, the lightbulb is now more than just a light-delivery system, and has become a 'designed' object in its own right. With the tonal quality of emitted light improving with these advances, so the exposed lightbulb has become an increasingly viable lighting option within of contemporary interiors. These new illuminants have offered up endless opportunities for experimentation and creativity to professional interior designers and amateur home-decorators alike.

Today, technological advancements within the lighting sector continue apace for instance; various researchers are looking into the potential of fibre-optic lighting, while others are trying to solve the problem of LED coating degradation due to heat, which in turn affects their emitted light quality and longevity. On average, around ten major breakthroughs in LED technology are happening each and every year. For example, researchers from the University of Illinois recently developed a new method of making brighter and more efficient green LEDs, while the California-based Ostendo Epi Lab has just debuted the world's first polychromatic GaN-based LED.

In the future, as the causal link between health and light becomes ever more established, so new more-healthful forms of lightbulbs will undoubtedly take centre stage. As new scientific research is revealing, the types of lighting we have been using for over a century disrupt our circadian rhythms, which has a consequential knock-on effect on our health and general well-being, yet we now have the scientific and engineering wherewithal to produce lightbulbs in the future that have purposes way beyond just illumination.

ETERNITY CHANDELIER BY LEE BROOM LED bulbs set within 'cabochon' caps on a gold-plated ring create a stunning halo effect (left).
TOM DIXON-DESIGNED Bespoke handelier in situ at No.2 Upper Riverside, London (opposite).
BESPOKE BULB-RING CHANDELIER Specially created by Northern Lights for 1901 Restaurant and Wine Lounge at the Andaz Hotel in Liverpool Street, London (overleaf).

A trend that's spreading wide + fast

The growing popularity of exposed lightbulbs and bulb-revealing fixtures can be explained mainly by their sheer novelty. Indeed, it is only with recent advances in lighting technology that exposed lightbulbs have finally shed their long-time inherent flaw: glare. But over and above this, the exposed lightbulb also seemingly represents the discarding of an older lighting tradition, which relied so heavily on the reflection and diffusion of emitted light through the use of shades. The stripped-down quality of exposed lightbulbs, by contrast, jives with the millennial penchant for openness and honesty – this is electric lighting reduced to its truest, most essential form.

The trend for bulb-themed lighting is also very much driven by the creative flexibility it offers. By using exposed lightbulbs in rows or clusters, or just stringing them randomly across a ceiling one can create stunning lighting effects that tend to give a space a sense of glowing warmth, contributing

A TRIO OF LIGHTS These Plumen 001 lightbulbs used with simple black sockets are shown in a coffee bar, but would work equally well over a kitchen breakfast counter (left).
HUDSON HOTEL IN NEW YORK Exposed lightbulbs twinkle, giving atmospheric warmth to Hudson Common, the welcoming industrial-chic, modern-day beer-and-burger joint set within this well-known mid-town boutique hotel (opposite).

SAYING HELLO Suspended letter lighting greets diners at The Whale Wins restaurant in Seattle, USA (opposite).

DENALI HAIR, TOYKO Salon interior, incorporating furniture by Artek, designed by Atsushi Osada / Milestone in 2016 showing an interesting use of minimalist bulb holders (right).

to a more relaxed casual-contemporary feel. And thanks to the inherent purity of their aesthetic, exposed lightbulbs are also stylistically adaptable. With a bit of intelligent design thinking, they can be used in virtually any space. For example, exposed lightbulbs can work well within the context of commercial interiors, especially in bars, restaurants, coffee shops and hair salons, as the accompanying imagery shows. This is undoubtedly due to their intrinsic no-nonsense functionality and stark but striking visual aspect.

The widespread use of exposed lightbulbs has also been accelerated by the fact that it is possible to design one's own bulb-bearing fixtures, albeit within the constraints of common-sense health and safety guidelines. The three interiors shown on this spread are good examples of how to create memorable lighting statements without a huge amount of cost. Here we find steel-framed, bulb-holding letters spelling out a friendly welcome; minimal wooden wall mounts providing a raw yet natural bulb-baring look; and a stunning assemblage of copper piping fashioned into a sculptural ceiling fixture – all of which goes to show that the bulb can be the star in any room. You just need to use a bit of design ingenuity to pull it off. In fact, today the idea of a bare illuminated lightbulb literally equals the opportunity for inspired creative expression.

DE EBELING IN AMSTERDAM One of the city's most famous cafés, redesigned by Framework in 2013, and now lit up by this stunning copper-pipe ceiling light (above).

MADE IN CAMDEN This stand-alone bar and dining room designed by Michael Sodeau is located at The Roundhouse in north London (opposite and above). It incorporates simple exposed lightbulbs to dramatic effect. The clever red wall fixtures not only provide direct lighting to the banquette dining areas, but also help to delinate the room's space, while the rows of exposed lightbulbs on the ceiling add a simple touch of understated glamour.

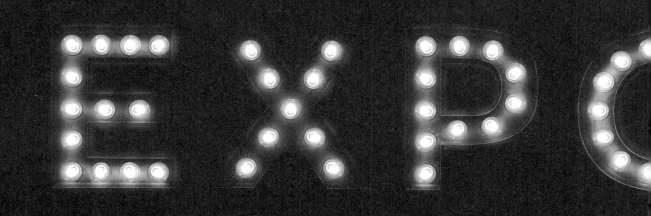

lightbulb types + fixtures

The simplicity of the bulb

The standard lightbulb is unquestionably one of the most iconic designs of all time and, when used by itself in an interior setting, can make a strong aesthetic declaration. Indeed, in our increasingly complex world there is something rather emotionally reassuring about the physical simplicity of a naked lightbulb. It is no coincidence that the latest editions of *Simplicity*, written by the lateral-thinking guru Edward de Bono, feature a graphic representation of a lightbulb on their covers. And while in times gone by the bare lightbulb spoke of utilitarianism, poverty and transience, today it has quite different connotations and speaks of an enlightened aestheticism that rejects the visual noise and emotional clutter of consumerist decadence. As such it is an intellectually strong yet visually understated interior design statement, which nonetheless can be surprisingly difficult to pull off.

KANT BULB HOLDER This simple socket cover by House Doctor comes in three metallic finishes and provides a dash of minimalistic lighting glamour (opposite).

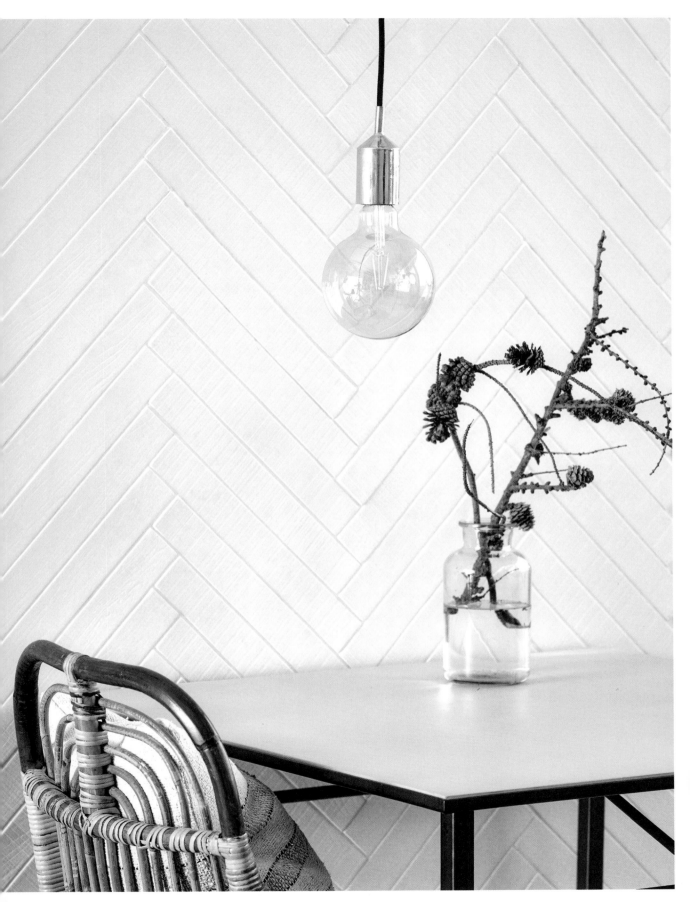

CORD LAMP A winning minimalist combination by Form Us With Love for Design House Stockholm, featuring a classic textile cord strengthened with steel tubing, a large bulb and a dimmer.

The basic bare-lightbulb-on-a-cord set-up can, if handled deftly, look surprising good in a variety of interiors for it has a quietly whispered purity that is the very antithesis of the many bold lighting statements available today. The main thing when trying to achieve this really quite refined style is to make sure it doesn't look like an unintended feature, as then it will just make your whole room look like an unfinished project. The way to ensure this doesn't happen is to make sure the rest of the room is finished to a high standard of spec. It also helps to use bulb holders that are not just your average white plastic fittings from the local hardware store, but rather have some intrinsic quality. There are actually a large number of simple holders now being manufactured that fit this bill, which have various coloured and metallic finishes. In some cases a single bare lightbulb hung from the ceiling can look great, especially when sited on a landing or in a hallway or some other small space. However, if you are planning to illuminate a larger room, you may well find that a single lightbulb could look a bit underwhelming, and may well not provide sufficient lumens for lighting functionality. As ever with lighting, it is all about context, so if you are planning to light a larger space, such as a kitchen, dining room or living room, then you may find that several bare lightbulbs in simple holders positioned in a row or in groups will give you not only the lighting levels you need, but also a better look, while still retaining that 'keep it simple' vibe.

Redolent with symbolism, the 'standard' lightbulb hanging from the ceiling has in many ways the quality of a found object – a sort of conceptual meta-design, if you like. Exposed lightbulbs can also work extremely well when used in conjunction with simple wall and ceiling mounts. The keeping-it-simple-with-bare-bulbs look can be used in all types of interior contexts, from period to contemporary, and can be achieved using a variety of different bulbs, from run-of-the-mill white bulbs, to oversized globular bulbs, to silvered halogens. The main issue is how the particular bulbs that have been selected relate to the ceiling or the walls on which they are mounted, and whether they are in overall balance with the room. Given this, trial-and-error experimenting is probably the best way to ensure that you've got the right number of lightbulbs positioned in exactly the right place. It really is that simple, but then again simplicity can sometimes be a very complex thing to achieve. And that's because simplicity is in many ways the ultimate form of sophistication.

The basic bare-lightbulb-on-a-cord has a quietly whispered purity that is the very antithesis of the many bold lighting statements available today.

1. pared-down

For nearly 130 years, the quintessential shape of the incandescent filament lightbulb did not really change. The reason for this was twofold. On the one hand, the classic bulb form was ideal from a technical standpoint because it allowed the delicate filament to be surrounded by an inert gas and protective glass casing, and this became industry standard. On the other hand, the harsh quality of the light emitted by traditional incandescent bulbs meant that generally they had to be shaded, so it didn't much matter how they actually looked. Likewise, fluorescent tubes and halogen bulbs were also produced in a set range of conventional shapes and sizes according to industry standards. The glare of all these different forms of lighting was generally regarded as just too unforgiving, with even softer 'pearl' options being, more often than not, used in conjunction with fabric shades or glass diffusers. Within the realm of lighting, virtually all the design effort went into the creation of lamps and fixtures that would soften the light emitted from a hidden bulb, so it would ultimately be easier on the eye.

E27 PENDANT LAMP BY MUUTO Shown in situ,
providing a pared-down Nordic simplicity (opposite).

E27 BY MATTIAS STAHLBOM FOR MUUTO This striking pendant naked bulb, which, according to its manufacturer, 'plays with the subtle aesthetics and simplicity of industrial design', is available in a wide range of colours.

O ver the last five years, however, things have changed radically and the creative focus within the realm of lighting has shifted towards the design of the lightbulbs themselves. Consequently, the range of lightbulbs available today has expanded immensely, thanks in large part to advances within lighting technology, especially with regards to more energy-efficient LEDs and halogens that boast better colour tones. In the wake of the various scientific breakthroughs that have occurred in the field of lighting, a number of new design-led bulb-making companies have been set up, and they now offer a dazzling array of bulbs that are aesthetically lights years away from the 'standard' lightbulb. Mirrored, faceted, twisted and sculptural, this new upstart class

of low-energy designer-illuminants are meant to be shown off – and can be used by themselves using simple bulb holders or within various bulb-revealing fittings and fixtures. One of the leading manufacturers in this area, Plumen, states that its mission is to, 'Inspire the adoption of efficient light technologies by creating beautiful-to-behold and beautiful-to-use lighting' that combine 'creativity, technology, design and art to establish a new exciting world of energy-efficient lighting for everyone'. Certainly, its range of original lightbulbs, including the distinctive looping 001 and its golden dimmable 003 LED pendant, have broken the age-old aesthetic mould and herald a more formally inventive and expressive tendency in the design of lightbulbs.

HEAVY METAL PENDANT BY BUSTER + PUNCH Available in a variety of metallic finishes (left), and shown in a kitchen setting in a no-nonsense row above an island countertop (below).

NORDIC MODERN A trio of Edison-style bulbs in Markslöjd's simple brass Sky holders gives this cool monotone Swedish interior a touch of warming *hygge* (opposite).

EDISON 1 WIRE PENDANTS BY INDUSTVILLE Available in brass, copper and pewter finishes, these are intended to be used with Industville's low-energy vintage-style LED Vintage Edison Squirrel Cage Filament lightbulbs.

Interestingly, in Scandinavia, more than anywhere else, there are a number of start-up companies working within this new field of 'designer lightbulbs'. This can, perhaps, be explained by the Nordic region's long-time fascination with the potential of lighting to bring a sense of warmth and character into interior spaces, and by the recent and widespread revival of interest in Scandinavian design. Manufacturers such as Muuto are typical of this interest in the creative use of exposed lightbulbs, with its minimal E27 socket suspension light holder being an especially popular choice for the display of this new crop of bulbs. These new companies also tend to offer their own bespoke bulbs. Indeed, a number of long-established design-led manufacturers are getting in on the act

too, with the historic Orrefors glassworks having recently launched an extensive range of lightbulbs, designed by that veritable matriarch of Swedish design, Ingegerd Råman, that scatter the emitted light in a very engaging and poetic way.

The successful incorporation of these design-statement bulbs within contemporary interiors is often best achieved when the actual holder is kept as unobtrusive as possible, so it does not deflect too much attention away from the main event – the actual lightbulb. These types of lightbulbs also often work very well when grouped together to create a central lighting statement, with clusters and rows of them being an easy way of producing a stunning lighting focus within

TRIBECA GROUP BY SØREN ROSE FOR MENU Inspired by the designer's own collection of vintage factory lighting, the Tribeca range of exposed lightbulb lamps has a sleek and sophisticated pared-down industrial aesthetic (this page and opposite).

a room, such as over a table in a dining room, strung over a counter island in a kitchen or falling cascade-like in a stairwell.

There are also an increasing number of minimal yet interesting bulb holders to choose from that can be used with ordinary low-voltage standard lightbulbs or with more visually arresting 'designer statement' ones, such as those produced by London-based bulb-maker Plumen and the Copenhagen-based design company Menu. The latter produces Søren Rose's Tribeca Series (including the multi-stemmed branch-like Franklin lamp holder), which was inspired by the designer's playful hacking of his own extensive collection of American industrial lighting from the early to mid-20th century.

Indeed, Rose's range of minimal bulb-holding fixtures has an industrial-chic aesthetic that looks good in virtually any interior.

Simple single pendants come with various holder options, from Buster + Punch's Heavy Metal, in a variety of finishes, to brightly hued choices that can be mixed and matched to a desired colour scheme. Even crown-mirrored bulbs, if utilized in an innovative way, can be used to create a striking stylistic effect within an interior. More than anything, the use of design-statement lightbulbs and simple bulb-revealing holders allows users a strong degree of mass-customization.With a degree of user creativity, this new clutch of designs helps to personalize spaces, while still giving that strong, on-point, 21st-century aesthetic.

SININHO SUSPENSION BULB HOLDER The youthful Portuguese design studio Studio Galula has cleverly used natural cork to create a functional and versatile fixture for Nedgis, shown here used with a vintage-style filament bulb in a bedroom setting.

SCANDINAVIAN IN ITALY Designer Marina Lund incorporates Achille Castiglioni and Pio Manzù's seminal Parentesi pole light into a Scandi-chic interior in Asolo, Italy.

2. vintage bulbs

Vintage-style Edison-type lightbulbs are a quintessential element and recurring theme of industrial-chic interiors, which in recent years have become a global phenomenon, having originally sprung from the hipster enclaves of Williamsburg in Brooklyn and Shoreditch in London during the late 1990s. This raw and unashamedly nostalgic look can be seen as an outright rejection of early 1990s over-considered minimalism, with its perfect but, frankly, emotionally sterile white cube-like spaces. It was also a make-do-and-mend reaction to the globalization of the international property market during the late 1990s and early 2000s, which saw homes and offices in the central areas of New York and London being speculatively bought up en masse by newly cash-rich overseas buyers as 'safe as bricks and-mortar' type investments. This fuelled a property boom, which consequently saw real-estate prices rocket in various districts of these cities, making them unaffordable for the young and the creative.

CUISINE A PARIS A modern French kitchen features a custom iron staircase that seamlessly ties in with the stainless-steel kitchen cabinetry, lit by a mix-and-match trio of suspended Edisonian bulbs (opposite).

This Italian manufacturer produces a range of interesting vintage-style bulbs (below and opposite) that will give an ambient warmth to almost any interior.

RETRO BULB This pear-shaped squirrel cage filament lightbulb by Dowsing & Reynolds gives a lovely warm glow and is perfect for low-lighting or mood-lighting contexts.

nevitably, inhabitants such as these were financially nudged out of the urban centres and into previously run-down boroughs. And like the nomads they were, this coterie of creative youthful individuals set themselves up, often temporarily, in abandoned shops, warehouses, and the like. And what is the easiest and cheapest way to light such re-thought spaces? A plug, a piece of electric cord, a bulb holder and a lightbulb, of course. And that was ultimately the genesis of the exposed lightbulb revival.

This hipster aesthetic reflects the post-industrial millennial zeitgeist, which hankers after authenticity in the face of an evermore digitalized, atomized and commercialized world. In terms of interiors, this means culturally appropriating 'original' artefacts

from the pre-digital era – which is viewed wistfully as a simpler, less complicated and more real time. One of the main leitmotifs of this 'new–old' look is industrial-style lighting, which provides a sense of utilitarian functional reliability. It gives spaces an engaging bygone aesthetic that helps engender an emotional connection, just like aged, worn antique brickwork and distressed wooden floors.

In response to this renewed interest in the industrial heritage of the past there are a number of specialist dealers, both in Europe and America, who sell period factory lighting. Likewise, online auctions are also a good source of original wire cage light guards and bulkhead fixtures, which have heaps more industrial salvage credibility than today's

WATTNOTT BY PLUMEN
A glorious shape-diverse group of retro illuminants that look great singly or when clustered (opposite).

plethora of vintage-style copies. Yet, as with anything, even when it comes to choosing retro style industrial lighting, personal purchasing choices are more often than not made according to convenience, availability and cost. So while original industrial fixtures tend to be very well made and exceedingly honest in terms of their use of materials and functionality, they will also probably be more expensive to acquire and will, in all likelihood, need rewiring by a specialist. But once someone gets into the antique lighting collecting habit, it can become quite an obsession, as original pieces provide such a powerfully authentic look. And that doesn't just mean old factory lights, for other kinds of antique lighting – from crystal chandeliers to Arts & Crafts-style Pullman lamps – look equally good when used with today's new crop of Edison filament bulbs. Original bulb-

revealing 'sputnik' lights, usually featuring multi-coloured enamelled holders, can also introduce a bona fide fifties flavour to a contemporary interior.

The numerous vintage-style Edison bulbs that are now available can also work equally well by themselves using simple holders – sans fixtures – and can be worked singly or together in a variety of assemblages. Each is slightly different from the next, as they echo the various historic patents held by the different original manufacturers. Today, there is a wide choice of period-type lightbulbs that channel these subtle variations, and when used together as an interesting mélange of different bulb sizes and styles, they can offer a strong visual curiosity to an interior. Thanks to their warm but relatively dim glow, you will often need more than one of these types

DIAMOND NO.1 CAGED PENDANTS These industrial-style fittings by FilamentStyle are available in six colours, for mixing and matching, and with a pendant cord option available too.

LED EDISON-STYLE BULBS BY INDUSTVILLE This London-based company offers six nostalgia-evoking bulb-shape options, as well as a host of vintage-style cages and fixtures to go with them (this page and opposite).

of bulbs to light up an average sized space sufficiently, so they are best used in multiples to form a loosely strung DIY-style chandelier.

Vintage-style bulbs can also look sensational when used in conjunction with the numerous cage-like guards available, which help enhance that hip retro-industrial aesthetic. These can likewise be used in rows or clusters to increase the volume of light so as to illuminate a space more fully and dramatically. Varying the heights of the different bulbs being used can also add extra interest to a lighting arrangement, while helping to make it a more customized solution. In fact, vintage-style Edison bulbs can transform almost any light fixture, large or small, old or new, by adding an evocative touch of old-fashioned charm. In addition, there are a large number of contemporary-

style transparent glass pendants, that have been specifically designed for use with Edison-type bulbs and have an appealing hybrid new-old quality. And for a completely different look, there are various Steampunk-style fixtures on the market, usually featuring gas piping, which can give an interior a quirky sense of intrigue.

If Thomas Edison were alive today, he would probably be completely bemused by our 21st-century obsession with his iconic incandescent bulb, considering that he was at the vanguard of technological progress. And yet the Edison bulb, with its warm glow, has perhaps more than any other object the power to evoke homely nostalgia – which, as any dedicated follower of interior fashion will tell you, is exactly what the current Scandinavian *hygge* lifestyle-obsession is all about.

3. bulbs with a twist

While vintage-style Edisonian bulbs are most commonly used to create a so-called 'rough-luxe' or industrial-chic aesthetic, there are a number of other recent bulb designs that instead channel a far less utilitarian aspect. These types of bulbs predominantly fall into two main categories: Design Statement illuminants, which have a strong contemporary aspect, or De-Lux twinkling dazzlers, which are unashamedly sumptuous and glamorous in demeanour. These diversely styled bulbs are the complete antithesis of the ordinary standard lightbulb, and while the former are largely, but not necessarily exclusively, marked by a Scandinavian-style simplicity, the latter tend to have over-the-top brilliance that knowingly references the luxurious crystal chandeliers of earlier eras. In addition, there are numerous bulb-revealing fixtures that have recently come onto the market that embody both these looks – the stylishly simple and the richly opulent – which can be used to transform an ordinary interior into an extraordinary space, as can be seen on the following pages.

DROP TOP These lampshades by HULGER for Plumen are a great way to showcase the already iconic Original Plumen 001 lightbulb, claimed by its manufacturer to be 'the world's first designer low-energy lightbulb' (opposite).

ORIGINAL PLUMEN 001 LIGHTBULBS A 21st-century energy-saving illuminant by HULGER and Samuel Wilkinson with a clever twist that has a 15W rating yet produces the same lumen levels as a standard 65W incandescent lightbulb.

In fact, one of the earliest manifestations of the Design Statement bulb, the TW003, was created by the Finnish designer Tapio Wirkkala in 1960, and has only recently been reissued by Artek. Looking as fresh as ever, this opaque diamond bulb ostensibly transforms the common lightbulb into an eye-catching light sculpture. The same could be said of the Plumen 001 bulb, one of today's most successful contemporary designs to fall within the Design Statement category. There are innumerable lightbulbs and bulb-bearing fixtures currently on the market that have a strong contemporary twist, giving them a playful sculptural demeanour.

The American cultural and political commentator Virginia Postrel once observed,

'Glamour is a beautiful illusion – the word "glamour" meant a literal magic spell – that promises to transcend ordinary life and make the ideal real. It depends on a special combination of mystery and grace.' And in many ways this is exactly what both Design Statement and De-Lux lighting do, casting magical illuminating spells over interior spaces so that they eclipse the everyday.

An early example of the De-Lux lighting aesthetic was the classic Hollywood style bulb-studded vanity mirror that became so synonymous with the dressing rooms of silver-screen starlets during the 1930s. This quintessential Art Moderne look has been endlessly revisited since, and indeed it remains a recurring theme in today's

TW003 PENDANT Seen here with a matching bulb by Tapio Wirkkala, this iconic light was originally designed by Finland's greatest form-giver in 1960. It looks amazing in this stalactite-like formation above a café counter.

CRYSTALED BULBS BY SELETTI
A great way of bringing a
touch of faceted jewel-like
sparkle to any living space.

bathroom and dressing room interiors. But there are now a host of other ways to create a sensational luxury look incorporating exposed illuminants, thanks to the recent emergence of a new breed of high-style De-Lux lightbulbs, many of which feature 'crystal' or faceted jewel-like globes.

Until relatively recently, it was financially unrealistic to manufacture these types of bulbs, but thanks to an exponential increase in the longevity of LEDs over the last few years, these products are now more commercially viable in terms of manufacturing cost versus overall lifespan. These novel, sparkling 'precious' bulbs can be used to add a touch of opulent brilliance to any interior. And in many ways they can be seen to function much like the twinkling crystal chandeliers of yesteryear, by scattering the emitted light in a prism-like fashion

through their cut-glass or faceted globes. Prior to gaslight and electrification, crystal chandeliers were used to enhance the rather feeble luminescence of candlelight. Today, it is difficult to fully comprehend the gloominess of interiors before Edison's invention of the first practical electric bulb. To give a little insight into this, just consider the light in your fridge or microwave, which represents more illumination than an entire home would probably have enjoyed prior to the invention of gas and electric lighting: the lumens emitted by a single candle equate to only one hundredth of the luminosity cast by a 100-watt bulb. And that is why painstakingly cut droplets of lead crystal were used to amplify, as much as possible, the precious light given out from a candle. Today's new bulbs do much the same work as antique chandeliers by refracting the rays emitted from their internal light source

FROSTED AND CLEAR CRYSTAL BULBS BY LEE BROOM
Taking their inspiration from the traditional craft of crystal cutting, these bulbs are designed to fit into any light fixture or just a simple wall mount, and can be hung singly or in clusters (this page). Set above a vintage kitchen table and six translucent Louis Ghost chairs by Philippe Starck (opposite), these sparklers give a touch of nostalgic glamour to an eclectic interior.

– in this case small LEDs rather than wax candles. These 'crystal' and jewel-like bulbs essentially disperse the light around a room, thereby creating evocative mood-setting pools of light and shadow. But over and above this, these new types of bulbs – such as those designed by Lee Broom – have their own inherent visual interest and can be seen to cleverly combine light-source and light refraction into a single unified entity.

There are also a number of bulb-revealing fittings and fixtures that give a luxurious look to interiors, ranging from various large ring-shaped suspension lights that hold a plethora of bulbs to simple minimalistic gold lamp holders that can be used in conjunction with oversized 'bulbs of interest'.

Since the 1950s, so-called 'sputnik' pendants, with their starbursts of bulb-holding stems, have also given countless interiors a ritzy spin, and continue to do so as there is now a new crop of ceiling fixtures that are their direct descendants. Likewise, using large-scale bulb-studded signage lettering – now available from any number of sources – can add 'up-in-lights' glamour to an interior. One of the most common faux pas when selecting lighting for an interior is to choose pendants or fixtures that are proportionally too small for the space they are intended to light. Given this, in terms of lighting, sometimes more can be more. So think Design Statement multi-bulb-display fixtures or twinkling clusters of De-Lux crystal bulbs that draw the eye to that most mood-evoking thing of all – light.

PLUMEN 003 (LED) FOR PLUMEN
This design was co-created by
the French jeweller Marie-Laure
Giroux and the British designer
Claire Norcross, and provides
both direct and ambient lighting,
shown below in situ.

BLOCK LAMP BY DESIGN HOUSE STOCKHOLM

Designed by Harri Koskinen, this lamp comprises a weighty, solid block of glass that encases a standard bulb as if it were ice, and comes in two sizes.

DIAMOND LIGHT BY ERIC THERNER FOR FRAMA Originally created in 2009, this diamond-shaped functional-yet-sculptural bulb was one of the very first 'designer lightbulbs'. It adds sparkle to this monotone-themed Scandinavian interior styled by Jenny Hjalmarson Boldsen (opposite).

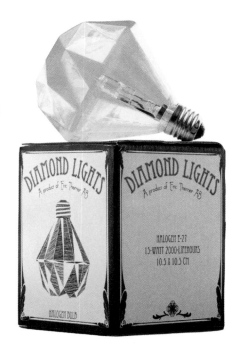

FLYTE MANHATTAN LAMP BY SIMON MORRIS This 'magical' bulb-shaped lamp uses magnetic levitation to defy gravity (left and below).

4. complex fixtures

In the early years of electrification, often quite complex lamps featuring exposed or revealed incandescent bulbs were used as a means of showing off this wondrous new invention of the modern industrial age. However, as electric lighting became more commonplace in the early years of the 20th century, so the electric lightbulb's novelty wore off and matters of functional practicality came to the fore. To this end, shades and diffusers were most often used to soften the dazzling light cast by electric lightbulbs in domestic environments, and it was not until the 1950s that the fashion returned for lighting designs featuring exposed or revealed bulbs. In 1954, Tito Agnoli led this new dare-to-bare trend with the launch of his Model 387 for Oluce, which featured a special Cornalux lightbulb that had a half-shaded globe, which could be used to direct the emitted light in a very precise way. This design heralded a new minimalistic aesthetic in Italian design and demonstrated how exposed lightbulbs, which were almost exclusively the preserve of factory lighting, could be used to create stylish lighting solutions for the contemporary interior.

TARAXACUM 88 S PENDANT LIGHT BY ACHILLE CASTIGLIONI FOR FLOS It looks as sculptural as the seating it has been twinned with (opposite).

STUNNING BULB CHANDELIER
Originally designed in 1988, the Taraxacum 88 S Pendant by Achille Castiglioni is a veritable icon of Italian design, as well as being one of the most eye-catching designer statement lights of all time.

F

ollowing Agnoli's lead, the progressive Italian designers Achille and Pier Giacomo Castiglioni created one of the most iconic lighting designs of all time: the Toio uplighter in 1962 (see page 156), which is essentially an assemblage of ready-made components, including a car headlamp. Eight years later, Achille joined forces with Pio Manzù and designed the innovative Parentesi pole light (see page 49). This piece used ceiling and floor mounts, and a taut suspension wire with a pivoting holder that allowed a large bulb to be height- and direction-adjusted. It was, however, Castiglioni's later Taraxacum 88 S of 1988 that was his most spectacular lighting design to feature exposed lightbulbs. With its mirror-polished aluminium faceted

holder housing 120 clear Globolux bulbs, this remarkable design provides both direct and indirect light, while giving any interior a strong focal piece.

Another well-known designer who over the decades has returned again and again to the theme of 'the lightbulb' in his work is the super-inventive German Ingo Maurer. Early on in his career, in 1966, he created the Bulb table/floor lamp, which took the form of a gigantic lightbulb that encased at its core a real mirror-crowned lightbulb. This Pop oversized meta-object was followed by a series of lightbulb-revealing fixtures that display Maurer's quirky playfulness, which include his Birdie's Nest and Birdie's Ring

BIRDS RANGE BY INGO MAURER

Birdie's Nest and Birdie's Ring chandeliers are bulbs-taking-flight fixtures. Providing an element of whimsical poetry to any interior, they are among Maurer's best-known designs.

85 LAMPS CHANDELIER BY RODY GRAUMANS FOR DROOG
One of the first manifestations of the dare-to-bare lighting trend, originally debuting in 1993, this classic New Dutch Design chandelier looks spectacular above a vintage display cabinet in this room by interior designer Billie Dainton (opposite).

chandeliers that feature 'flocks' of low-voltage lightbulbs adorned with white goose feathers.

The one lighting design in particular that can be most plausibly credited with kicking off today's craze for exposed luminaires, however, is Rody Graumans' 85 Lamps chandelier, which debuted in 1993. Rough-and-ready, this assemblage of bulbs, wires and connectors continues to be manufactured by Droog Design, and still gives any interior a special standout quality. When it was first launched in the mid-nineties, 85 Lamps was not only one of the earliest designs to herald the experimental and exploratory New Dutch Design movement, but it also powerfully demonstrated how an opulent lighting

design could be achieved by creatively using 'found' off-the-shelf parts.

Graumans' design, however, did have an important precursor in the sublimely elegant form of the 2097 chandelier designed by Gino Sarfatti in 1958. This super-stylish suspension light comprises a simple brass pole from which 30 arms radiate outwards in order to support 30 cabled bulb holders. Although a relatively complex structure visually, it is testament to Sarfatti's genius that this lighting design exudes such a strong sense of minimalistic sophistication. Indeed, the 2097 can be seen as a glorious manifestation of postwar Milanese design at its super-stylish best. By taking 'found' lightbulbs and

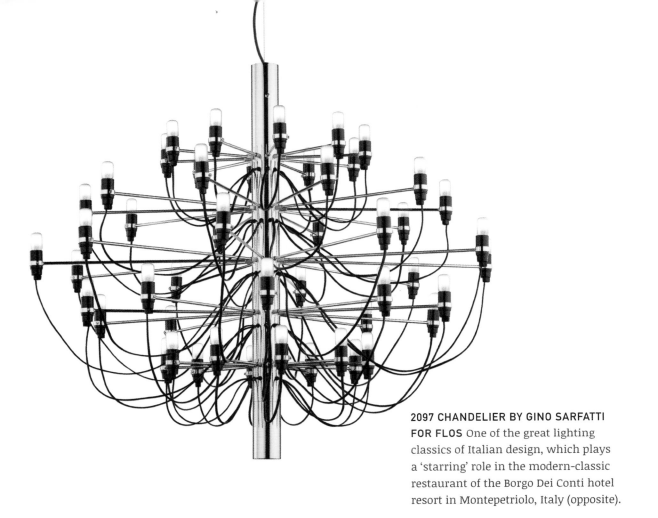

2097 CHANDELIER BY GINO SARFATTI FOR FLOS One of the great lighting classics of Italian design, which plays a 'starring' role in the modern-classic restaurant of the Borgo Dei Conti hotel resort in Montepetriolo, Italy (opposite).

transforming them into what is ostensibly a stunning light sculpture, Sarfatti managed at a stroke to expunge the lightbulb of its previous utilitarian associations, thereby lighting the way for other designers to experiment creatively with the simple lightbulb within their designs.

Another more recent bulb-themed design that has similarly attracted much international acclaim is Harri Koskinen's Block Lamp of 1997 (see page 69), which is today recognized as a Finnish design classic. This deceptively simple yet aesthetically sophisticated design takes the form of a rectangular block of glass that is cast in a mould and encases an ordinary lightbulb, which nestles in between the two

halves of the ice-like moulding. It looks great on a table or on a shelf, and lights up any space with its seemingly magical quality.

Over the next few pages you will find other stylistically diverse bulb-focused designs, which are aesthetically far removed from the simple bulb-and-cable set-ups found in some of the other chapters of this book. These are fixtures that display lightbulbs in all their glowing glory, and while many have an inherent complexity, it is paradoxically only a means of celebrating the lightbulb's innate simplicity.

CERO S3 AND CERO S5 PENDANTS BY SOTTO LUCE Understated and minimalist, these clever clusters of three or five bulb holders come in five finishes, while their power cords are available in eight different colour options, allowing for a degree of personal customization (left and above).

MASS LIGHT PENDANT BY NORM.ARCHITECTS FOR &TRADITION Inspired by street lighting in Paris, Barcelona and New York, Kasper Rønn and Jonas Bjerre-Poulsen designed this simple bulb-style pendant in 2012, which can be used on its own or in a cluster (opposite).

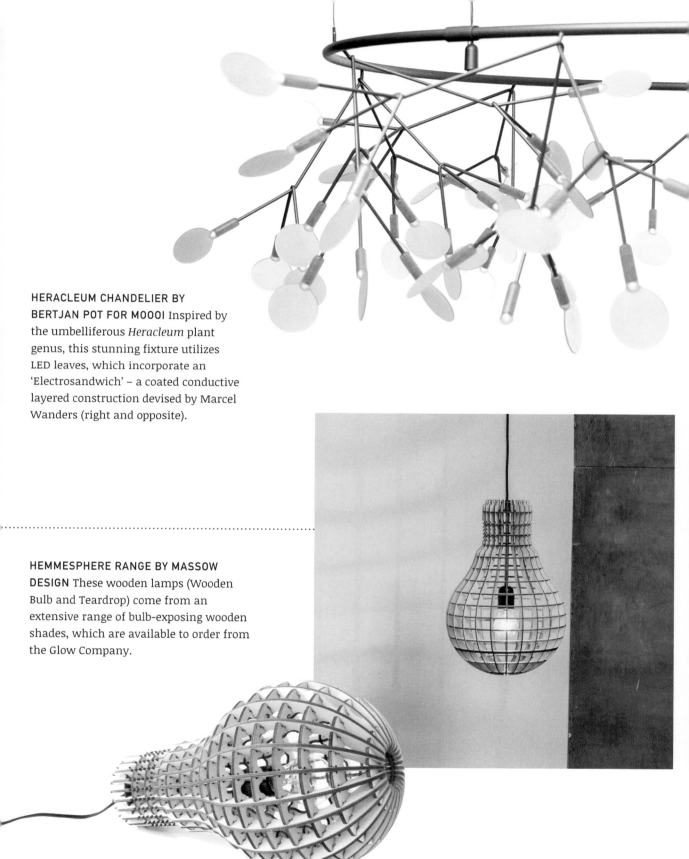

HERACLEUM CHANDELIER BY BERTJAN POT FOR MOOOI Inspired by the umbelliferous *Heracleum* plant genus, this stunning fixture utilizes LED leaves, which incorporate an 'Electrosandwich' – a coated conductive layered construction devised by Marcel Wanders (right and opposite).

HEMMESPHERE RANGE BY MASSOW DESIGN These wooden lamps (Wooden Bulb and Teardrop) come from an extensive range of bulb-exposing wooden shades, which are available to order from the Glow Company.

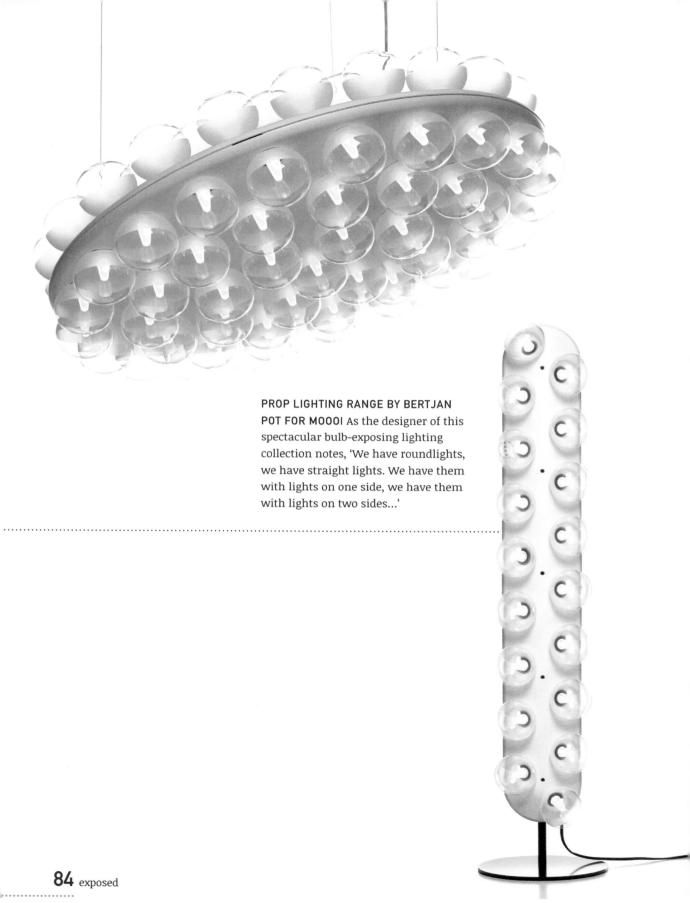

PROP LIGHTING RANGE BY BERTJAN POT FOR MOOOI As the designer of this spectacular bulb-exposing lighting collection notes, 'We have roundlights, we have straight lights. We have them with lights on one side, we have them with lights on two sides…'

5. design hacks

Today, there are numerous on-line retailers as well as bricks-and-mortar stores that can help you get actively creative with your own bespoke lighting solutions. Not only is there now a vast array of lightbulbs to choose from, but also an impressive range of different power cables, too – for instance, the Italy-based supplier Factorylux produces 50 different woven fabric lighting cables in a rainbow of attractive hues. Likewise, there are all sorts of other bits and pieces on the market to help you customize your lighting solutions, from various holders – available in Bakelite, ceramic, brass, bronze, silver nickel-plate and even nine-carat gold plate with hooked or cord-grip connectors – to all sorts of diversely shaped bulb cages, which again are available in a huge variety of coloured and metallic finishes. The range of galvanized conduit pipes and accessories currently available is similarly impressive, as is the number of alternative styles of ceiling roses with single and multiple outlets.

One can also use simple strands of lightbulbs in innovative ways to create sensational focal points in a room or a garden – for example, a string of bulbs tacked randomly to white-painted brickwork can look amazing, as can a string of lights loosely strung across a patio area. A minimal bulb-cable-and-plug set-up can also be used in a variety of ingenious ways – for example, combined with nautical rope or tree branches to create attention-grabbing assemblages. You will see arrangements such as this over the coming pages.

Even a simple wall-mounted bulb encircled with marigold yellow paint can look outstanding if you are using it in the right interior context. Other clever hacks could include using 'found' objects from bottles to stepladders in your lightbulb assemblages. But apart from the freedom to create your own personalized lighting statements, this new and widening crop of lighting hardware allows one to rethink the illumination of spaces – for instance, to shed light on a dark stairwell you can just loop a stranded caged light around a banister for a quick and easy fix. Likewise, an eye-catching Kinfolk-style floor light can be easily thrown together using a bulb, a holder and some flex that is supported on a crook-like iron hook hammered into a simple stabilizing base made of solid wood. In fact, this do-it-yourself dare-to-bare lighting aesthetic offers a host of exciting design possibilities – so enjoy scoping out what's available in terms of kit, and relish the creative challenge of making and amending, while always remembering to heed lighting safety guidelines.

A ladder library

This clever design hack featuring a distressed wooden ladder and a caged lightbulb holder provides an easy and affordable shelving solution that has a strong industrial-retro vibe.

Festoon garden lighting

Transform your garden seating area at night with the addition of a string of lightbulbs (suitable for external and internal use) artfully draped to give a festive firefly-like effect – these examples are from House Doctor.

Yellow spots

An easy-to-achieve yet ingenious paint hack that transforms simple exposed lightbulb wall fixtures into warm glowing pools of light. Devised by interior designer Lachlan Stewart, they look especially good when used on roughly plastered rustic walls, as seen here.

Vintage luminaries

A super-simple and super-clever design hack idea from
IKEA: take some vintage lamps, discard their fussy shades
and add some different sized and shaped IKEA bulbs for
an interesting lighting arrangement.

Island task

This French kitchen, designed by architect Romain
Thévenot, features a clever lighting hack. A pair of
double-cabled looping socket holders with interesting
striped bulbs are used as task lighting over an island
counter, while providing a touch of retro-industrial chic.

Silver birch chandelier

Bringing a bit of outdoors inside, this clever chandelier is made from roughly nailed-together branches of silver birch wrapped with a strand of simple lightbulb. It creates an impactful centrepiece in this Swedish kitchen designed by Jimmy Schönning.

Nautical
stair lighting

This wonderful lighting
assemblage was designed
by Patrick Crawshaw for
the stairwell of a house in
Bath, England.

Standard reading lamp

An oh-so-clever-yet-ingeniously-simple design hack by Stéphanie Boiteux-Gallard combines a block of natural wood as a base with a standard wrought-iron hooked pole stem, onto which is loosely strung a simple cable-and-socket set-up.

Wardrobe lighting

Kikkerland's Pull Cord Light Bulb is an inexpensive yet useful way to illuminate the dark corners of a closet space with its LED Edison-style bulb.

Stateside lighting carousel

The owners of this renovated schoolhouse in Pittsburgh, Pennsylvania, strung a series of cabled lighting cords with traditional Edison bulbs around a black metal ring in order to create a central focal point in the living room.

Scandinavian yuletide vibe

Sparsely needled pine boughs attached to a string of bare bulbs give a cool yet festive Scandi look to this table setting, featuring pine twigs and pine cones, alongside white candles and simple pottery wares – all from House Doctor.

Cluster of light bubbles

This dramatic lighting assemblage,
comprising twelve E27 holders and bulbs
from Muuto, gives a strong focal point
to this kitchen interior and imbues it with
a playful spirit.

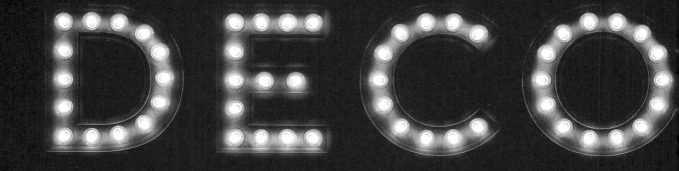

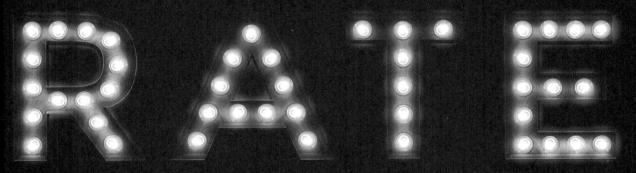

RATE

living with lightbulbs

a practical guide to decorating with lightbulbs

Decorating with exposed lightbulbs or bulb-revealing light fixtures and fittings is a great way of adding interest and mood to an interior, as well as getting that stylish 'contemporary-retro' vibe. But before you start stringing up Edison lights or buying expensive design-statement, bulb-revealing chandeliers, it is important to think of the interior context in which you are planning to use them. For instance, would one type of lighting style be more appropriate than another, given what you already have to work with in terms of that specific space? Do you want the lighting you are going to introduce to an interior to stylistically complement or contrast with what already exists? What functional requirement does the lighting need to have? Or is it purely going to be used to provide a room with a warm and homey atmosphere? And do you want it to be the centrepiece in a room, or something much more subtle?

NEW NORDIC LOOK Mattias Ståhlbom's iconic E27 bulb holders for Muuto are used in an eye-catching row configuration, their heights playfully adjusted by tying simple knots in their cords. They are shown alongside Iskos-Berlin's bio-composite Fiber chairs, also by Muuto (opposite).

Maybe you are starting the design of an interior from scratch – just the blank canvas of plain walls. If so, then it is a good idea to think of building up your interior scheme in layers, as any professional interior designer would do. The first layer of your palette would be your so-called 'spec', which basically means everything that is physically stuck down in an interior. This would include the type of flooring you want to use, plus any ceiling or wall treatments such as paint, brickwork, stonework, stucco, corking or panelling. Then the next layer of your interior palette would be colours and textures. Once you have determined those, it is time to start on the third layer, which involves deciding what types of larger furnishings should be used to fill the space – which is where your lighting decisions come into play. The final fourth layer of your interior scheme is its 'dressing', meaning the strategic selecting and placing of works of art, decorative objects, books and other items of interest to finish off 'a look'.

Despite this simple step-by-step interior design strategy, all too often lighting is treated as an afterthought within an interior scheme, despite it being one of the most important elements of a room in terms of its ability to create warmth and mood, as well as visual

STUDIOUSLY SCANDINAVIAN

This charming high-ceilinged space, designed by Copenhagen-based H. Skjalm P., features the company's simple satin-finish brass bulb-holding pendant, which is hung low to provide an increased sense of intimacy (opposite).

interest. In fact, the quality of your lighting – both the physical fixture and the light it emits – is crucial in giving an interior its character or personality. Often an interior can be let down purely by a light fixture being of poor quality or not stylistically fitting in with the rest of the furnishings in a room. Quite simply, clever lighting can emotionally light up an interior. But over and above that, lighting can also affect your health and sense of well-being, so it is important to make sure, especially when you are using exposed lightbulbs within a room, that the light emitted is neither too harsh nor too dull as both can lead to eye-fatigue.

Given this, it makes sense to think of lighting as the fourth dimension of interior design and to give it the considered respect it deserves. This means using, where appropriate, a mix of different lighting to achieve the desired mood and light levels. So while you can have a stunning statement piece – whether in the form of a cluster of crystal bulbs or an enormous bulb-displaying fixture – as the focal point of your lighting landscape, you may well find it looks even better when supported with subtler, warm-toned lighting accents, achieved by using concealed light sources strategically placed to enhance the main illuminating attraction.

While you can have a stunning statement piece as the focal point of your lighting landscape, you may well find it looks even better when supported with subtler, warm-toned lighting accents.

ELECTRIFIED STEAMPUNK CANDELABRA This lamp made of electrical conduit pipes screwed together provides a quirky, old-world charm (opposite).

UBIQUA LAMP BY SELETTI Inspired by the handled work lamps of yesteryear, this lamp (available in bright yellow or bright green) is functionally versatile and has a useful hook on its side, so it can be suspended almost anywhere (top left).

MONKEY WALL AND TABLE LIGHTS BY SELETTI These tongue-in-cheek designs hark back to earlier lamps that were all about displaying the wondrous invention of the electric lightbulb (top right).

GREEN STAR WALL LIGHT BY ARGENT & SABLE Providing an eclectic big-top bohemianism to any room, this handcrafted lighting statement is made from reclaimed wood and incorporates authentic 'circus lights' (right).

If one decides to go down the 'nothing but the bulb' route – meaning using bulbs with just simple holders – then there are a number of exposed lightbulb looks that can be achieved, ranging from minimalist to maximalist and from vintage to retro to contemporary.

If you decide to go for vintage-style Edison 'filament' lightbulbs, make sure you let them visibly stand out, as they can add a spectacular and nostalgic industrial twist to an interior. Even bare fluorescent tubes can look stunning in certain interior schemes with a bit of creative decorating magic, but it always comes down to the context of the location. So a lighting idea that looks amazing in an apartment building corridor or in a hotel lobby might not translate so well into a domestic environment, not just because of the different functional requirements of a residential living room or a kitchen, but also because of differences in scale.

Another consideration is ceiling height, which might seem obvious, but time and time again you see lighting that is positioned unsympathetically. For example, if a room has very high ceilings and large windows that flood it with natural light, then probably artificial lighting is only going to be required in the evenings, so you will want to position fixtures in such a way that they do not visually interfere with the natural light coming into the space. Also, be mindful about

CB0213 WALL LIGHTS BY HOUSE DOCTOR This pair of brass swinging lights with their oversized bulbs are arranged in a stepped manner, thereby providing an interesting wall feature (opposite).

The best way to approach the lighting of a room is first to work out your ambient lighting requirements, then focus on your accent lighting, and then finally consider your potential task lighting needs.

where you exactly site wall fixtures, especially if you want to hang artwork on your walls now, or possibly at some point in the future. Certainly, if a room is underlit, then it can dramatically reduce the impact of a canvas hanging on a wall. One of the easiest ways of building versatility into your lighting scheme is by going to the extra trouble of having dimmer switches installed, because then you can adjust your indoor light levels during the day in accord with the light levels outside. The best way to approach the lighting of a room is to first work out your ambient lighting requirements, then focus on your accent lighting, and then finally consider your potential task lighting needs – all of which could take the form, in one way or another, of exposed lightbulbs. The main thing about today's plethora of stylistically diverse lightbulbs is their incredible functional versatility and their seemingly endless potential for imaginative experimentation, as the examples illustrated on the following pages show. Just as Edison's original incandescent lightbulb lit up our homes over 100 years ago, so today's fresh set of bulbs has opened new doors of possibilities within the realm of contemporary interior design. So take pleasure in exploring this exciting and illuminating world and enjoy even more getting actively creative with it.

CB0150 PENDANT BY HOUSE DOCTOR This brass pendant with its amber-toned globe bulb looks especially good when hung low over a dining table (opposite).

DESK LAMPS Kayan 3-D printed shades by Formaliz3d, twinned with Plumen's 001 bulbs, provide an interesting new take on office lighting (far left).

FOCUSED LIGHTING A CB0213 wall light by House Doctor – in this instance used singly – is intended to provide direct task lighting for reading (left).

TABLE LAMP BY H. SKJALM P. The simple blackened metal frame of this architectonic Danish bulb-baring lamp gives it a strong minimalist-yet-sculptural aesthetic (below left).

Consider what your light fixture needs to do. For example, does it need to provide enough direct light so one can read by it, or see what one is eating at a dining table, or navigate a staircase safely?

DESK LAMP WITH GD0208 LED BULB BY HOUSE DOCTOR Comprising a cabled, oversized ambre-lustre bulb and a science-lab-chic adjustable stand, this do-it-yourself assemblage offers precise task positioning (left).

POLE LIGHT IN A CABINET OF CURIOSITIES A London interior designed by Hubert Zandberg incorporates a retro-looking, bulb-baring light with a multi-coloured stem (opposite).

a walk through the home

Thanks to the range and versatility of the different bulb-themed lighting solutions now available, it is quite possible to use them in every room in the home. In fact, you just need to assess carefully what style of bulb-light would suit your chosen space best. This means thinking specifically about the main purpose of the room you are planning to illuminate and how light – that all-important fourth dimension – can be used functionally, as well as setting the desired atmosphere. For instance, a kitchen will have very different lighting requirements from a bathroom or a home-office. On the coming pages you will find interiors from all over the world, many created by leading designers and architects, which have been grouped according to the different types of rooms found in a home. It is hoped that the resulting walk-through guide will provide helpful inspiration for how to use exposed lightbulbs and bulb-revealing fixtures in a host of creative ways.

A STRING OF BRIGHT PEARLS Simple stranded lightbulbs add a touch of DIY glamour to the studio of American wood artist, Ariele Alasko (opposite).

living
rooms

While the fashion for decorating with bare bulbs first emerged in the neo-bohemian studios and coffee shops of millennial-trendy Brooklyn and East London, today there are numerous design-led manufacturers, mainly found in Scandinavia, who are producing bulb-baring designs that are often more deluxe than rough-and-ready, and as such are probably more suited to domestic interiors. In terms of living rooms, if you have high ceilings, then a dramatic bulb-bearing chandelier can work really well as an interesting central lighting focus. Multi-bulb fixtures or a cascade of bulbs can likewise look great when sited in corners, where they can provide a focus of visual interest in an otherwise dark nook. They can also be used to help functionally delineate space in this way, too, by creating cocooning areas within a larger space. One can also go down the retro route, as there are now numerous dealers specializing in original vintage lighting as well as a large number of 'design classics' still being produced, which can, if used thoughtfully, provide a living space with a definable sense of designer cachet.

A VOW OF SIMPLICITY
Stylist Marina Sinibaldi Benatti uses dropped socket fittings to enhance the monastic calm of this interior in Piacenza, Italy (right).

WIREFLOW CHANDELIER BY ARIK LEVY FOR VIBIA
This mathematically inspired bulb-bearing 3-D fixture reinvents the classic chandelier and eloquently defines the spatial dimensions of the room (opposite).

A CASCADE OF GLOWING BULBS
Muuto's omnipresent 'new classic' E27 fixture is used to create a dramatic lighting statement, showing this design's incredible versatility (previous pages).

TABLE LIGHT BY H. SKJALM P. An evocative pastel-toned sitting area is given a touch of Danish *hygge* with this simple black metal lamp used in conjunction with a warm glowing oversized bulb (opposite).

DIY01 PENDANT BY HOUSE DOCTOR These gigantic glass bulb-bles provide an interior with a strong feeling of ethereal lightness (right). They are threaded onto the fabric cable and then lit by a single electric bulb of the same size and shape.

TRIBECA FRANKLIN CHANDELIER BY SØREN ROSE FOR MENU Channelling utter Scantastic simplicity, this asymetrical chandelier has a delightful Nordic quirkiness (right)

MULTI-COLOURED SOCKET CHANDELIER Interior designer Claire Canning makes clever use of different primary-colour bulb socket covers to create this stunning centrepiece for a stylish new build in Norfolk, England (overleaf).

BACK TO THE FUTURE Emmanuel Renoird
used an original stainless-steel bulb-holding
lighting system to create this funky '70s-style
games room in France (opposite).

FUTURISTIC ILLUMINATION Here, Renoird
utilizes four Pantonesque bulb-holding panels
in order to create a space-age vibe (below)

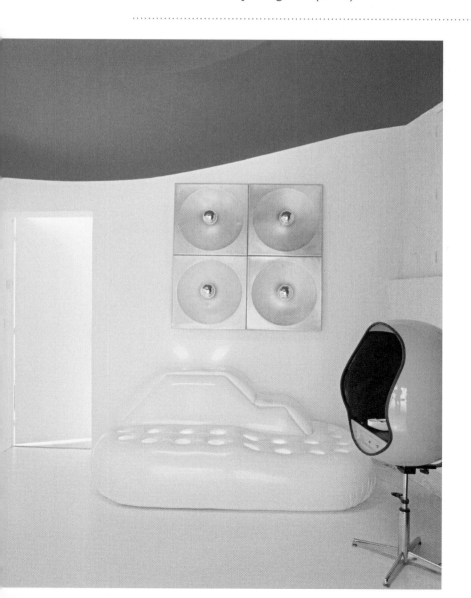

HEAVY METAL PENDANT BY BUSTER + PUNCH Creating a dramatic lighting feature at the Villa Minale, this exposed bulb design is traditionally worked at designer Massimo Minale's studio in East London (left).

MARBLE LIGHT BY STUDIO VIT FOR &TRADITION Made from white Italian Carrara marble and mouth-blown borosilicate glass, the pure geometric shape of this design gives it a strong artistic presence (opposite).

Suspended bulb lighting can be hung low to create a sense of intimacy in larger rooms or in spaces with very high ceilings.

Bulb-baring table lights are another useful way of creating a sense of light and warmth within a living room space, while additionally providing a certain degree of tasking functionality.

A MASTERPIECE OF MILANESE DESIGN The Lampadina table light by Achille Castiglioni incorporates a clear globe that has been partially sandblasted to help the diffusion of light. It also has a base that cleverly stores any excess cabling (opposite).

DANISH SIDE LIGHT BY H. SKJALM P. This stylish and versatile lamp from one of Copenhagen's leading design-led lifestyle stores is offered in raw brass, polished brass or a black finish (right) .

CONCRETE AND BRASS TABLE LIGHT With its use of raw materials and channelling of Scandi simplicity, this eye-catching illuminant by House Doctor gives a decidedly Nordic atmosphere (left).

BLOCK OF LIGHT While Harri Koskinen's Block Lamp works well as a side light on a table, as shown here (left), it works equally well when used on the floor functioning as much as an attractive illuminant as a quasi meta-art object.

CONTROL TABLE LIGHT BY MUUTO An interesting reimagined version of Muuto's E27 bulb-holder, this solid aluminium light with its playful control has an endearing no-nonsense sensibility about it (opposite).

kitchens
+ dining
areas

SWEDISH KITCHEN BY BALLINGSLÖV Cleverly lit with a pair of simple wall-mounted bulb holders and a pair of vintage-style bulbs set in copper sockets on long black fabric cables, the kitchen's retro-industrial theme is continued with the copper-pipe pan and utensil hanging racks (opposite).

KAYAN 3-D PRINTED SHADE BY FORMALIZ3D Designed to go with Plumen's new-generation bulbs, this provides a soft, sinuous shape that complements the curved silhouette of Plumen's 001 bulb (previous pages), also shown with Drop Top shades in a warm-toned, over-hob lighting feature (above).

KEEP IT RAW This neo-brutalist varnished concrete kitchen in Marrakech, Morroco, was designed by architects Studio KO and features a classic halogen bulb for industrial-chic illumination (opposite).

A LITTLE LIGHT RELIEF This stylish blackened metal and brass bulb holder, with its unusual woven cord by H. Skjalm P. can be used to provide useful task lighting within a kitchen environment (below).

It goes without saying that kitchens need to be lit properly so food can be prepared safely, while dining areas need a sufficient degree of illumination so that people can actually see what they are eating. Indeed, much of the enjoyment we take in food is down to what it looks like on a plate, so it is important that lighting over a dining table is neither too low-level nor too glaring. Similarly, in a kitchen area, specific preparation and cooking zones can benefit from being task-lit using simple bulb-holding fixtures, whereas other types of countertop spaces might be better lit by concealed lighting strips. When it comes to choosing bulb-type lights, there are styles to suit practically any kitchen or dining space, with the former usually best accommodated in simple holders used on their own or in rows, whether vintage-style or sleekly modern.

BULB STRIPPED BARE
A simple standard switched socket with a vintage-style bulb looks just right in this 'ancient and modern' kitchen in New Jersey designed by Smith-Miller + Hawkinson Architects (opposite).

ALPINE LIGHTING Two simple bulb holders give a utilitarian charm to this mountain refuge designed by Dévanthery & Lamunière in Valais, Switzerland (this page).

BRIGHT WHITE LIGHT A Form pendant, designed by Form Us With Love for Design House Stockholm, is shown in a Scandi-cool interior featuring other designs by Design House Stockholm (this page).

SPIKY RETRO PENDANT An attention-grabbing starburst pendant with twinkling bulbs helps enhance the '70s glam look of this contemporary Kensington interior, designed by Michael Reeves Design (opposite).

CB0150 PENDANT BY HOUSE DOCTOR This brass bulb-holding fixture comes with a 3-meter (9-foot) cord for easy height adustment, and looks fabulous when slung low above a small dining table, giving a special feeling of intimacy (opposite).

LOW HANGING CAGE This Sangkar metal cage by Tudò & Co is intended to give a modern and minimalistic Scandinavian-style aesthetic, with its cage form offered in five different shape options (this page).

RETRO COLLECTOR'S LOOK A vintage starburst fixture with its multi-coloured enamelled bulb holders is used to give a little bit of '50s panache to this shamelessly retro dining area (opposite).

1950S KITSCH WALL LIGHT Different-coloured bulb holders are matched with lightbulbs of the same hue, shown in a contemporary chalet in Cortina d'Ampezzo, Italy (below).

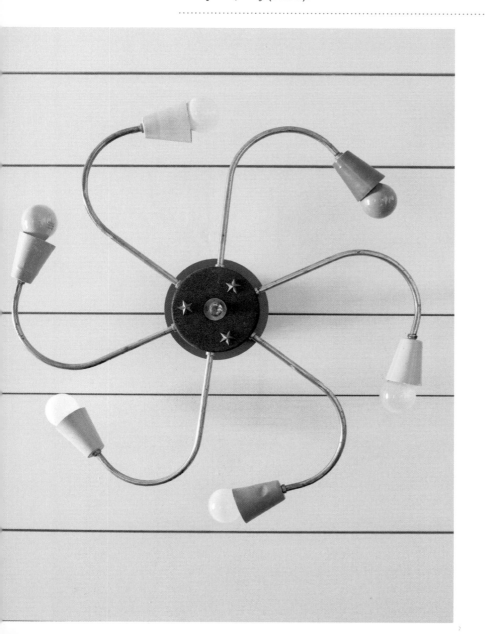

BULBS IN A TANK This unusual glass tank-like bulb-revealing light fixture complements the rustic table beneath, in the cool-toned interior of a modern mansion flat in London designed by Turner Pocock.

MONOCHROME DINING Styled by Michelle Halford, this graphically accented set-up features Menu's brass rod and bare bulb Tribeca chandelier (opposite).

MASS LIGHT PENDANT The body of this street-light-inspired design by Norm Architects for &Tradition is made from milled and polished white or black marble (above) or spun and polished brass or copper, which is then left to patinate naturally to brown and greenish hues respectively.

DROPLETS OF ILLUMINATION Muuto's
E27 socket suspension lights with
oversized bulbs are pitch-perfect when
used in conjunction with the Nordic
design company's Split table and Fiber
chairs (opposite).

SPIDER LAMPS BY FILAMENT STYLE
These cable-and-socket lights are
easy to customize to personal interior
requirements and come with either red
or black fabric cables (above).

To achieve the optimum
level of illumination
in a dining area, think
about using an oversized
solo bulb suspended
quite low, or alternatively
try a multi-bulb fixture
or a cluster of cable-
and-socket bulbs set
at a higher level.

DROP HAT SHADES BY PLUMEN A spectacular cascade of light, used in conjunction with Plumen's U-shaped 002 bulbs (opposite).

GLOWING BALL OF LIGHT Taraxacum 88 S pendant by Achille Castiglioni is the perfect statement for illuminating stairwells.

TRIPPING THE LIGHT FANTASTIC
Tom Dixon's Void Surface wall lights
spectacularly light up a staircase in
an apartment in Metropolitan Wharf,
London, designed by Dixon (below left).

GILDED FLOWERS OF LIGHT A hallway
designed by Collett-Zarzycki features
beautiful flower-shaped wall lights
with mirrored bulbs (below right).

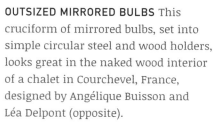

OUTSIZED MIRRORED BULBS This
cruciform of mirrored bulbs, set into
simple circular steel and wood holders,
looks great in the naked wood interior
of a chalet in Courchevel, France,
designed by Angélique Buisson and
Léa Delpont (opposite).

All too often hallways are an afterthought in interior schemes,
yet they are hugely important in setting the look and feel of
a residence. Entryways are the first 'welcome' visitors get to
your home and, as they say, first impressions always leave
the most lasting of impressions. Given this, it makes sense
to think of a hall as a gallery space and to light it accordingly
with one of the stunning exposed lightbulb options now
available, which will give it not only an identifiable character
but also an important sense of place. Likewise, landing
areas and stairwells can benefit from the use of this type of
lighting, whether it is a single Edisonian lightbulb, simply yet
judiciously placed, a twinkling cascade of new-style bulbs or
an acknowledged design classic.

One of the most important ways of making lighting work to best effect in hallways and stairwells is to ensure that the aesthetic of the chosen lighting solution fits stylistically with the space in which it will be placed, whether it is an industrial-chic, concrete-walled lobby area or a wooden panelled corridor in an Alpine ski-chalet. Indeed, as with most things that relate to interior design, context is everything.

WALL-WASHING WITH LIGHT Achille Castiglioni's iconic Toio floor light for Flos is used to great effect in this raw concrete hallway (this page).

LIGHTING THE WAY Muuto's Control lamp helps brighten the way in this clever staircase-cum-closet (opposite).

OUTDOOR WALL LIGHT This glazed
bulb-revealing fixture perfectly suits
the stripped-wood aesthetic of this
contemporary mountain cabin in
Haute-Savoie, France, designed by Hélène
Roux and Léa Delpont (opposite left).

ORLANDO CYLINDER WIRE CAGE Setting
a nostalgic tone with the use of one of
Industville's cigar-shaped Edison-style
filament bulbs (opposite right).

REGENCY MODERN This modern
bulb-bearing wall light makes passing
reference to the carriage lights of
yesteryear (above left).

PIERRE VINTAGE PENDANT LIGHT
This bulb cage from MY Furniture
has articulated wire 'petals' that can
either be positioned hanging downwards
(above right) or 'opened' to create a
flower-like bell form.

STRIPPED-DOWN FIXTURE A simple antique-style, brass bulb holder looks perfect in this Lower Eastside retro interior, especially with the houseplant suspended from it to provide some natural greenery and brighten up this urban hallway (below).

ALMOST INVISIBLE This simple socket and bulb adds a touch of sophisticated simplicity to the fabulously tiled landing area of this historic building in Marrakech, Morroco, designed by Agnès Emery (opposite).

bedrooms

EFFORTLESS COUNTRY LIVING This simple cable and switched socket make an excellent bedside lighting solution.

I RICCHI POVERI FIVE BUTTERFLIES LIGHT
This limited edition Ingo Maurer design makes a stunning bedroom light when set against a mural, with its winged insects hovering in the dark around the glowing bulb (below).

CLEAN, WHITE AND BRIGHT A bedroom in Spello, Italy, designed by Paola Navone, with a modern four-poster bed flanked by two minimalist bulb-bearing floor lights (opposite).

While the function and nature of other rooms in our homes change according to new patterns of living, the bedroom as a place of quiet solitude remains a constant. Indeed, it could be argued that the simpler a bedroom is, the more likely it is that it will provide the peaceful calm we all seek as a refuge from our increasingly technologically connected world. And what better way to create this much-desired sense of monastic simplicity than to use uncomplicated bulb lighting to set the tone.

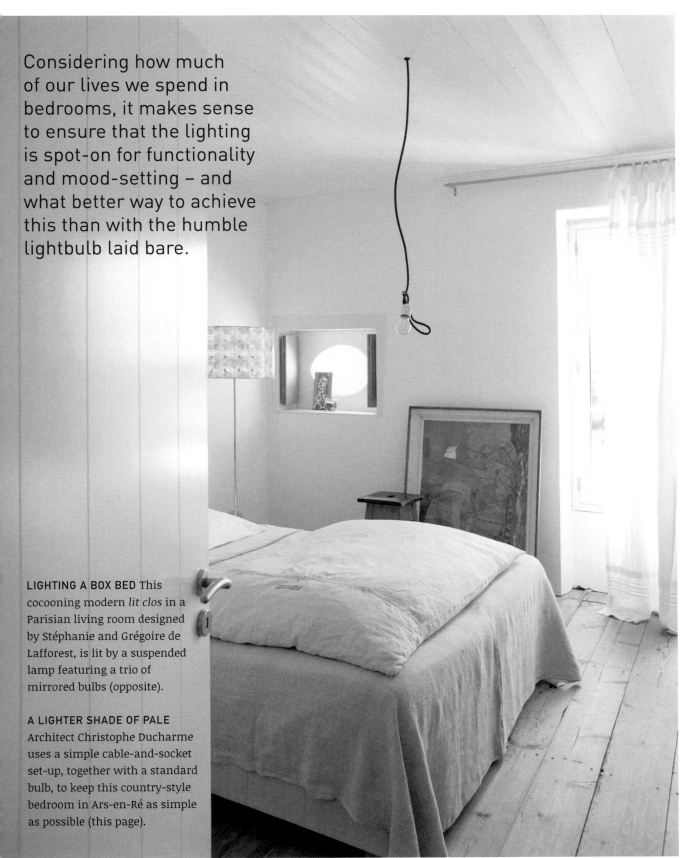

Considering how much of our lives we spend in bedrooms, it makes sense to ensure that the lighting is spot-on for functionality and mood-setting – and what better way to achieve this than with the humble lightbulb laid bare.

LIGHTING A BOX BED This cocooning modern *lit clos* in a Parisian living room designed by Stéphanie and Grégoire de Lafforest, is lit by a suspended lamp featuring a trio of mirrored bulbs (opposite).

A LIGHTER SHADE OF PALE Architect Christophe Ducharme uses a simple cable-and-socket set-up, together with a standard bulb, to keep this country-style bedroom in Ars-en-Ré as simple as possible (this page).

Indeed, there are various clever ways to achieve an atmosphere of purity and calm within a bedroom using exposed lightbulbs, as the various interiors in this section attest, and certainly having an inbuilt switch on a socket can help with the functionality of bulb-lights used for bedside illumination. Whether you are aiming for a sense of cool tranquillity or a feeling of heartwarming repose, there are different bulb options available that will help give you the specific tonal qualities desired for your very own sanctuary of quiet ease.

NORTHERN LIGHT Broste Copenhagen, a purveyor of Danish *hygge* since 1955, uses a concrete globe-bulb holder to shed light on a bedroom (left).

A BIT OF LIGHT RELIEF The Cero S5 pendant light by Sotto Luce provides a touch of warmth and glamour in this predominantly neutral bedroom (opposite).

AN EDISIONIAN TANGLE
The Edison 5 Bulb Cluster from Lights4fun adorns a wall of The White Room studio, Fitzroy, Melbourne, styled by Lynda Gardener (this page).

TWISTS OF LIGHT Two Plumen 001 bulbs, suspended on simple holders, flank the bed in this striped white and pale blue interior (opposite).

LIGHT ON WHITE Super-simple curling cable and an oversized globe bulb look perfect in this rustic Greek bedroom (below).

HARDWORKING ILLUMINANT This useful wall light with multi-USB socket and dimmer is designed by James & Thedin for Markslöjd. It makes the perfect bedside light as it can also be used to charge a phone overnight (opposite).

bathrooms

HOOKED UP Design House Stockholm's Work Lamp by Form Us With Love looks great in this historic bathroom, suspended on arrow hooks from the same company.

MIRRORED BULBS Three reflective bulbs are set into natural stone panelling in the washroom at the Alto restaurant in Hong Kong, designed by Tom Dixon (below).

CAGEY LIGHTING A bathroom in a historic loft in Vancouver features a pair of cages for over-the-sink illumination (opposite).

When it comes to lighting bathrooms, it is a good idea to think in terms of layers of illumination, starting with general ambient lighting, then more focused atmospheric treatments and then, finally, close task-lighting options, such as those needed for shaving or applying make-up. More than anything, however, it is absolutely essentially to use commonsense and to ensure health and safety legislation is strictly complied with, so as to avoid any potential problems with electricity and water.

MONASTIC SIMPLICITY A converted convent in Capri designed by Giuliano dell'Uva employs a simple bulb-and-cable set-up to illuminate this modern-meets-ancient bathroom (opposite).

WORK LAMP This versatile lamp by Form Us With Love for Design House Stockholm, inspired by the caged factory lights of yesteryear, is hung low to provide an intimate feel (right).

SIMPLE BRASS HOLDER This metallic fitting sets the scene in this bathroom designed by Tarkett, featuring an unusual carpeted wall that looks like patterned concrete (below right).

What is surprising is just how well the various bulb lighting options now on offer suit such different stylistic contexts. Whether it is the tranquillity of a bathroom in a converted Italian convent or the masculine sophistication of an on-trend, industrial-chic New York washroom, the bulb is the star.

BLOBULAR RELECTION A mirrored bulb in a white holder looks perfect in a bathroom in Spello, Italy, designed by Paola Navone (above).

STRICTLY VINTAGE A pair of old-school brass wall lights with Edison-style bulbs look perfect in the washroom of a historic country house in West Sussex, England (opposite).

THE MODERN BATHROOM SINK A trio of stylish bulb holders provide the illumination over the basin in this bathroom designed by Joao Botelho / WA+G Architects (below).

INDUSTRIAL-CHIC BATHING A marble and aqua-green-tiled shower room designed, by Elizabeth Roberts Architecture & Design, New York, features a black metal four-bulb wall-fixture that gives the room a sophisticated masculine edge (opposite).

Index <small>Page numbers in *italics* refer to illustrations</small>

MARBLE LIGHT BY STUDIO VIT FOR
&TRADITION The base of this table
light (which can also be used as a
pendant) is made from milled
and polished marble, while its
glass bulb is mouth-blown from
thin borosilicate glass.

Resources

UK & Europe

&Tradition
www.andtradition.com

Artek
www.artek.fi

Buster + Punch
www.busterandpunch.com

Design House Stockholm
www.designhousestockholm.com

Dowsing & Reynolds
www.dowsingandreynolds.com

Droog
www.droog.com

Factorylux
www.factorylux.com

FilamentStyle
www.filamentstyle.com

Flos
www.flos.com

Flyte
www.flyte.se

Frama
www.framacph.com

Gods Own Junk Yard
www.godsownjunkyard.co.uk

Heal's
www.heals.com

H. Skjalm P.
www.hskjalmp.dk

Hay
www.hay.dk

Holloways of Ludlow
www.hollowaysofludlow.com

House Doctor
www.housedoctor.dk

IKEA
www.ikea.com

Ingo Maurer
www.ingomaurer.com

Industville
www.industville.co.uk

John Lewis
www.johnlewis.com

Lee Broom
www.leebroom.com

London Lighting
www.londonlighting.co.uk

Menu
www.menu.as

Miljø Interior
www.miljo-interior.com

Mr. Resistor
www.mr-resistor.com

Muuto
www.muuto.com

Nedgis
www.nedgis.com

Northern Lights
www.northern-lights.co.uk

Plumen
www.plumen.com

Seletti
www.seletti.com

Sotto Luce
www.sottoluce.com

The Conran Shop
www.conranshop.co.uk

The Glow Company
www.glow.co.uk

Tom Dixon
www.tomdixon.net

TwentyTwentyOne
www.twentytwentyone.com

Vibia
www.vibia.com

US

Beam
www.beambk.com

Bulb Concepts
www.bulbconcepts.com

Cedar & Moss
www.cedarandmoss.com

Crate&Barrel
www.crateandbarrel.com

Design Within Reach
www.dwr.com

Just Bulbs – The Light Bulb Store
www.justbulbsnyc.com

Kikkerland
www.kikkerland.com

Target
www.target.com

China

Tudò & Co
www.tudoandco.com

Picture Credits

Selected Bibliography

Dietz, M. + M. Monninger, *Lights, Leuchten, Lampes*,
Taschen, Cologne, 2005

Egan, D. + V. Olgyay, *Architectural Lighting*,
McGraw-Hill, Boston, 2002

Fiell, C. + P. Fiell,
    1000 Lights, Vol.1, 1879 to 1959, Taschen, Cologne, 2005
    1000 Lights, Vol.2, 1960 to present, Taschen, Cologne, 2005
    Masterpieces of Italian Design, Goodman Fiell, London, 2013

General Electric Co. Ltd, *The Story of the Lamp*,
The General Electric Co. Ltd., London, c. 1920

Kron, J. + S. Slesin, *High Tech: The Industrial Style and
Source Book for the Home*, Allen Lane, London, 1979

R. Lenk + C. Lenk, *Practical Lighting Design with LEDS*,
Wiley-IEEE Press, Hoboken, NJ, 2017

Myerson, J + J. Hudson, *International Lighting Design*,
Laurence King, London, 1996

Pavitt, J., *Brilliant: Lights & Lighting*,
V&A Publications, London, 2004

Powell Morgan, A., *The Pageant of Electricity*,
D. Appleton-Century Co., London + New York, 1939

Stross, R.E., *The Wizard of Menlo Park: How Thomas Alva Edison
Invented the Modern World*, Three Rivers Press, New York, 2008

Szenasy, S., *Light: The Complete Handbook of Lighting Design*,
Running Press Book Publishers, Philadelphia, PA, 1986

EXHIBITION CATALOGUES
Vitra Design Museum, *Ingo Maurer: Light – Reaching for the Moon*,
Weil am Rhein, 2004

Vitra Design Museum, *Lightopia*, Weil am Rhein, 2013

Acknowledgements

We would like to express our appreciation to all the people involved in the realization of this beautiful book. Firstly, we would like to thank Eszter Karpati for coming up with the book's concept and then commissioning us to write it. Many thanks must also go to Helen Bratby for her stunning graphic design work and to our editor, Sian Parkhouse, for her good-natured management of the project. Likewise, we are grateful to everyone who has worked in-house on the project, especially Emma Heyworth-Dunn for her scheduling management, Joe Hallsworth for providing helpful captioning information, Maeve Healy for overseeing the book's high-quality production and, of course, Jacqui Small. who made a number of key inputs during the book's crucial gestation. We are also much obliged to Sarah Smithies for helping us source additional imagery. And, lastly, we would like to acknowledge the wonderful contribution made by all the lighting designers, interior designers, architects, photographers, manufacturers, design-led retailers and picture libraries who have so kindly loaned us imagery – a very big thank you to you all.

KEEPING EVERYTHING IN SUSPENSE
Marble lights by Studio Vit for &Tradition, here showing two of the seven different models from this classically inspired geometric range (opposite).

SP1000/1/2 SOCKET COVER BY HOUSE DOCTOR This funnel-shaped bulb holder is available in various different brushed metallic finishes, and provides an element of Scandi cool to any interior. It can be used on its own or in groups.

THE KINFOLK TABLE

THE KINFOLK HOME

29

30

31

32

33

34

36